Witchcraft and Monsters

A Collection of Poetry

Kala Godin

Copyright © 2019 by Kala Godin

First edition January 2019

Book design by Adriatica Creation

ISBN 978-1-988902-29-6 (paperback)
ISBN 978-1-988902-30-2 (ebook)

Published by Patchwork Press
https://www.facebook.com/KalaGwrites/

Contents

Part one:

On Witchcraft

Witchcraft

Your god
Has never known me.
And I,
Don't care to know him.

I've never known
Any religion that isn't
Sharp teeth and sickly sweet smiles,
Dirty nails and blood stained cotton.

Those with blind eyes,
See all.
Those who don't speak,
Sing.

I'm part Destruction,
Chaos and Fear,
Love and late night,
Slurred truths and not shy,
Dream and Nightmare.
One hundred percent Goddess.

Those who can't move,
Fly.
Those with no power,
Will be the Final Judgment.

I worship the Goddess inside.
The one who sits between my ribs,
And sings to my heart.
The one who speaks like me.
Reminding me when to be kind,
And when to spit venom.
The witch Goddess in me,
Who refuses to be burned.

Necromancy

I keep
Raising the dead,
Like it's going out of style.

Raise dead feelings,
Dead issues,
Dead ideas.

The dead see,
The Dead Sea,
And weep red.

And I,
Release the dead,
Because I'm dead tired of them.

Love Potions

I'm the kinda girl
That mixes love potions
For other people.
Never using them for myself,
Never needing to.

It's like I've got
Love poems running through my veins,
Instead of blood.
Like I've got Rose Quartz
Always in my pockets.

Look at the way
I fall in love with everything I touch.
Something new everyday.
Look at the way I love,
The idea of love.

The idea of
Every cliché.
Like kissing in the rain,
Like reckless hands,
Like whispering,
"I love you,"
Before falling asleep.

Look at the way
I wear my heart on my sleeve.
Like I'm not scared
Of heartache.

Look at the way
I will sing heartache to sleep,
Tell it a bedtime story,
Tuck it in.
And love again,
The day after.

Predator

They tell me
I'm more witchcraft than girl.
More wolf than woman.
Like it's a bad thing
To be the predator,
And not the prey.

Like I should be a passive thing.
Like I should be a soft thing.
Like soft things don't bite.
Like passive things won't put hexes on people.

They say,
"Be quiet girl,"
"You're a loud one,"
"Don't you know your place?"
"God will save you, girl."

Like I'm not saving myself.
Like I want to be
Someone's silent, pretty decoration.
Like I want to be quiet.

They forget I carry cemetery dirt in my pockets,
And I burn my bridges,
If I have to.
They don't know that I wear charms,
Around my neck.
And whisper enchantments.
They hate that I wear
The title "Wolf," like a crown.
Like I'm anything other than the predator.

Snake Charmer

Sometimes,
I wish I could speak like summertime,
Speak like sweetness,
Speak like songbird.

Somehow instead,
I speak like snake charmer,
Speak like sway,
Speak like silence.

Speak like a sacrifice,
Speak like fire starter,
Speak like sin.

Pyro

I love aggressively.
I set myself on fire,
And let everyone watch as I burn.

When the fire has gone out,
I pick my ashes up,
And put them in my ribcage.

I ask myself,
"Why did nobody burn with me?"
The answer is always the same.

I don't know love in small doses.
I know how to spill my entire being out.
I know how to love completely.

And they fear me,
The way they fear the ocean,
The way they fear a wildfire.

I am too much of myself for them,
But never enough,
Of what they want.

Devil's Candy

l.
Maybe I like the way that darkness is always on my mind.
The way everything is haze and power,
And grit and grace and harsh.

ll.
It feels like silk,
Or a broken sob,
Or a lovers mouth.
Sometimes it's all of your demons playing nice,
Or maybe they all gang up on you.

lll.
It tastes like honey.
And bittersweet.
And chocolate with a touch of chile.
It tastes like sin on Sunday.

And snake venom,
And stardust.
And maybe they're the same damn thing.

Summoning

A scream,
A caw,
The ancient words no longer spoken.
The sound my feet do not make,
When they don't touch the earth.
A thank you sung from the lips of the nearly dead.
A fog to hide me.

Labyrinth

The entrance is a collection of broken bones and hanging vines
growing white little flowers.
I don't know if I've ever had a broken bone.
My rib aches occasionally, making me wonder if maybe I did and
just didn't realize.
Right is too bumpy. The ground is a patchwork of cobblestones and
potholes that would jar my arms and make me useless.
The walls tend to grow faces. Sometimes they whisper things like
"burden."
Some flash grins of gemstone teeth.

Call me Sin

They say that gods equal beauty,
but I am wrenched and unholy.
Unhealthy and dying.

Mortal to the very definition of the word.
I am too much for my body.
Too much glory that it rips at the seams.

I am waiting.
Waiting for my lungs to burst,
An explosion of stardust screaming.

Waiting.
For blinded eyes,
And all seeing.

I am waiting,
For twisted limbs flailing.
For unorganized dance.

Waiting.
For my wings to not catch wind,
For my fall.

I am waiting,
For my throne of bone,
Blood, and ash.

Waiting.
Until the gods kiss me,
And recognize me as one of their own.

Part two:

On Immorality and Fairytales

I Hold Olympus in my Palm

I'm like Apollo,
In the way the sun is stuck in my throat.
I know how to turn my light off,
But I will not close my mouth.
I will not risk burning myself.
Instead I will burn others.

I'm like Persephone,
I will smile at the angel of death not like a friend,
but instead like a lover.
This is not a prison.
This is a new way to grow.

I'm like Hermes,
In the way I wander.
No one place is home,
They all are,
So long as the ones I love are close.

I'm like Melinoe,
In the way I see life and death,
Like a family reunion.
In the way that I am chaos.

Flying

She sings to the moon at night,
Hoping,
Praying,
Begging,
Thinking that the moon will go to sleep.
Maybe Selene will take the night off.

Maybe Apollo would see the wax wings
She's melted onto her back.
See the way she craves him.

She was always the girl who loved too quickly.
So easily.
So all-consuming.
A gentle girl who loved too fiercely for a human.
A love that outshone the sun.

And Apollo watched her from the sky.
Kissing her cheeks when no one was watching.
Seeing her but seeing a mountain that he would climb.

She was so bright.
He'd never loved anyone before.
Made sure of it.
He didn't love her either.

She sparked so easily.
And she loved it.
Loved him.
And he liked watching her burn.

"Wings,"
He said.
Wings,
She carved.

The next day she flies,
He watches the way she sets herself on fire.

Sees the way she likes flying and falling,
And burning.

But he didn't tell her about the drowning.
She didn't sign up for the drowning.
He just wanted to be the brightest again.

The Big Book of Mythology

Tell me,
Does gun metal taste like
Blood shed?
Tell me if it's worth it.

This is not justice,
It is murder.

Tell me,
Why does Hera wait for her husband,
When she knows he's in the bed of another?

This is not love,
This is loyalty.

Tell me,
Why does Icarus burn with the sun,
When he knows that the moon is a tender lover?

This is not devotion,
This is pain.

Tell me,
Why does Aphrodite look for love in men with broken hearts,
When she can't possibly know what hurt is?

This is not compassion,
This is arrogance.

Bone Queen

Remember the leather pants?
The dark eyes, red lips, spikes,
Wild woman hair with messy waves and braids.
The outfit that makes me feel dangerous.

Remember that it makes me feel like I'm Persephone,
Looking for more magic than what was given to me.
Remember that it's not the outfit.

I'm picking out pomegranate seeds,
I laugh because the juice looks like blood.
I eat more than six seeds,
Persephone only ate six.
I want more than six months on a throne in the underworld.

I'll remember to wear the outfit.
Eat more than six seeds.
Take the whole damn castle as mine.

Millennial Warfare

We are the indestructible fragilities,
The unconquerable glass sculptures.
Humans waging wars against gods.
Living in a life we call disaster.

We are the so called arrogant,
The not-so-ignorant,
And undeniably immutable.

Living in a world so terribly small,
And yet so full of horror.
We beg the universe for help,
And we've never received an answer.

A broken planet is just being placed in our hands.
We are ordered to fix it.
Asked why we destroyed it in the first place?

The Fall of Angels

They were blinded by each other.

Whenever he left her, she could taste him like sin on her lips.
Her toes curl and her fingers tingle.
Her heart races and the thoughts in her mind spin like a vicious
whirlwind.
And every thought is centered on him.
When she first saw him,
She realized everything she had ever been told,
Was a lie.
When he first touched her,
A gentle kiss.
It was like everything she was
stopped completely,
Or maybe it sped up and she just didn't know the difference,
Maybe she just didn't care about the differences anymore.
Because hell,
She felt so *alive.*

Whenever he left her, he could still see her.
She was so goddamn beautiful.
Her smile was brighter than the sun.
He hated the fucking sun before he met her,
But he was addicted to her smile.
She was an open book.
Usually he'd consume her and move on.
But he couldn't do it,
Not to her.
Not with this feeling blooming in his chest.
Not when she brightened every time she saw him.
Not when he loses his breath when he sees her.
He couldn't break her for fear of breaking himself as well.

Ophelia

Ophelia tells herself that she can't swim. But the water is only at her
knees, if only she would stand up. There's not enough space.
She tells herself that love doesn't exist, but then she's falling and then
she can't breathe. And it's just like the drowning all over again.
Sometimes she thinks about him so much that she forgets her own
name. But that's not normal right? That's obsession, right?

She remembers the girl she used to live by.
A girl that turned into a woman overnight.
She turned into a woman but lost herself at the same time.
Her name belonged to the man she married.
Her life became caring for him.
Only him, only him.
There is only him now.

Ophelia thinks that love is claustrophobic.
It will squeeze her smaller until she's gone.
Ophelia wants to be anything but the damsel.
Ophelia wants to take up space.

She runs the bath.
She finds a pond.
A lake.
A river.
Space, she needs space.

He makes her feel small.
Tells her she's gained weight...But...
He loves her.
Says it like he's not sure.

Not enough space.
The bath?
River?

He holds her too tight.
Fingers digging until he finds bone.
Says "This is my fiancé."

Doesn't say her name.
Maybe he forgets it.
No one asks for it anyway.

More space…

She finds herself at the ocean one day.
She doesn't stop moving towards it until salt water is filling her.
Closing all the holes he dug into her.

She doesn't want to be saved.
Doesn't want to be the damsel.
Or the Fiancé.
So she'll teach herself how to be a tsunami instead.

Dishrag Daughter

Cinderella, they tell you that you are soot and ash
Dish rag and bastard.
Maid, sister, maid, sister.
MAID.
Not quite human.
Not human like them anyway.
Just an object.

They want a prince,
And you want anything other than the 4 walls of pain that stare at
you.
You want to take up space.
You want freedom.

So when they leave the house and fill their guts with riches,
You disappear,
To see a prince who would rather run away with you.

Man Versus Beast

She is told she is dangerous.
At 10 she thinks it's a joke,
At 17 she knows it's true.

She is too much.
Too quiet, until she is too loud.
Too pretty and too smart for this small town.

All of her books talk of adventure,
And a kind of danger that has nothing to do with her.

There are legends of a monster that lives in the abandoned castle,
But there is nothing more monster,
Then the man she's meant to marry.

Too many nights,
Too many men get rowdy.
Too much liquor in their veins,
Never enough thought in their brains.

Ten men leave,
Armed with torches and anger.
The next evening only three return.
Terrified and sober.
The town isn't ever concerned.

She knows where the castle is,
Everyone does.
She isn't scared of it,
She is scared of the man who will soon share her bed.

So she leaves,
Too quiet and unheard,
And then too loud when she knows that it wouldn't matter.

She makes a home out of a castle.
Carves a man out of a beast.
Makes a home out of him too.

The danger was never herself.
Never the books she loved,
Only the townspeople who now hunted her.

The monster was never the beast.
Never the forest he hid in.
Only the man who now lead the hunting party,
Only the man she was promised to.

Teeth

Red Riding Hood girl,
Giving out smiles to strangers.
Innocent smiles like sunshine.

Some men think they are wolves.
Sometimes they will look at you,
Like you are their Last Supper.

But they aren't starving,
And people aren't food,
And a smile isn't a, "Yes please."

So when you are walking alone,
And a wolf greets you with too much sly and not enough soft,
Show him your teeth and tear him to shreds.

Part three:

On the body

Dear Broken Body,

Sometimes I forget how to love you,
Sometimes I downright refuse to.
You don't always make it easy,
You know?
But I'm sorry,
And this is my thank you.

Thank you for making me take up space.
So many people are trying,
To shrink themselves.
And I only know how to grow.

Sometimes I can feel my sand running out,
Each grain falling from between my fingers.
You have taught me that the world is not always kind.
That life is not kind.
And this has taught *me* to be kind instead.
This has taught me how to smile at everyone.

You have given me more than I admit.
So thank you.

Sincerely,
The not always grateful girl.

The Tale of a Gorgon

Medusa and I?
We "get" each other.
...Even though I'm terrified of snakes....

And it's not,
Because I dyed blonde to blue.
But because,
People refuse to look me in the eyes.

Like somehow,
Looking directly at my wheelchair,
Is going to turn them to stone.

Like somehow,
Against all reasonable thought,
And science,
Looking at me,
Could cause them to get the plague.

Which doesn't even make sense?
That's not how life works...

But still they,
Pull away their kids,
Tell them not to stare,
Tell them not to even look,
Tell them not to ask.

They tell them,
Tragic stories.
Tell them,
To be careful.
But the tragedy,
Will never be caused by us.
The tragedy is us.

Ache

My body screams with ache.
Ache in my mind,
My ribs,
My lungs, my shoulders.

Ache of too much weight.
Never enough space,
But plenty of empty.

Contraction and Expansion

They say there is a fine line between fear and respect.
I am not saying that I disrespect my body,
But I am scared of the way it betrays me.

I respect it for keeping me alive this long.

But every year is a new adaption.
My muscles are almost non existent.
And my tendons are contracting,
Tightening.
I fear the loss of mobility in my one working hand.

I fear that eventually I will lose my voice.
Because it is the only thing that is mine.
And,
I'm holding the moon in the base of my throat,
But I no longer know how to move the ocean,
I know how to spill myself into it.

I'm afraid that eventually my jaw will lock itself shut,
And I won't show the moon the ocean ever again.
Instead I will swallow it,
And have to learn how to feel too full.

There is enough space in my body for the universe,
But my body doesn't know how to carry itself.

Spending my Borrowed Time

Listen to the quiet body raging,
Listen to the silence of my no movement swaying.
See the way my body doesn't know how to carry itself.
Doesn't know how to walk.
But knows how to feel,
All the aching and tender,
And sore, sore,
So damn sore.

And oh god,
The panic,
When my fingers don't want to work.
When they just won't grasp anything.
Those are the days I get scared.
Because I lose things that aren't even mine.
Because this is my borrowed time,
And I'm spending it too quickly.
Because my body is costing me too much.

Witching Hour

It's the 3 am sweltering heat,
Of too many blankets.
It's eyes flashing open.
Eyes dry,
Close and open again.
It's the foggy mind,
Forgetting I can't sit up.
Trying to.

Panicking.
Can't sit up.
Can't move, why can't I move?

Then I'm fully awake,
What was I thinking?
I've never been able to move much.

It's watching shadows move across my roof,
Body not moving,
But was flying in my dreams.

It's laying in the heat.
Knowing the demons don't sleep under my bed.
The demon is the always awake thing,
Making my body slowly weaker.
The demon is the 2 minutes of foggy brain,
Thinking it can move.
Desperately trying to move.

The witching hour brings the nighttime doom.
The "try to move."
The "you can't."
The "You can almost feel it though, can't you?"
"Can't you?"

Dear 17

Quiet girl,
Plucking pain from your veins.
Stop reheating the wounds,
Like they are leftovers.
They don't taste like memories,
They taste like loss, like forgot,
Tastes like rot.

Soft girl,
Quit pulling threads from your bones.
Stop trying to sew yourself,
Into someone new.
Because changing your appearance is easy,
But you can't rearrange the furniture of your head so simply.

Love from,
19

Lullabies for the Body Dwelling Monster

"Shh"
It's quiet again as the monster settles. Sitting pretty, Big smile.
Just like I taught her.

I only let her roam when pen hits paper or when the others have gone
to sleep.

The older she gets, the quieter she gets.
She gets smaller and bigger,
All at the same time.
Becoming less of a separate thing.
Becoming more of myself.

I know she doesn't mean it.
Doesn't mean to cause me the pain.
Doesn't mean to make my fingers contract.

She just doesn't know better.

She doesn't like the way people look at me.
Stare, or avoid eye contact?
She hurts just as much as I do.

I let her,
Cry sometimes,
Then I remind her that this isn't so bad.
We still have lots.
I tell her that we still have time.

So she settles back down,
And goes to sleep.

Part four:

On bad ideas

Old Poems in New Clothes

I know that I've written this poem before,
A few times actually.
You'd think it'd be old news by now.

But I'm well acquainted with all the ways,
My heart knows how to shatter.
All the ways it spills itself,
All over everything.

I'm well aware of all the ways that I know heartbreak.
So in-tune with the aches and echoes.
And I think I like it this way.
Always having to pick up my pieces,
Never putting them back together.

Pity was his Only Power

Ask this question,
Is there a difference,
Between pity and empathy?

Don't fall in love with the boy,
Who says no.
He thinks he's a god.

Ask him if,
He's with you because he feels like he has to.
Is there an unspoken,
Responsibility. . .

A duty that screams in his head,
"I love you! I love you, but only because no one else will."
He sees you as a broken thing,
A fragile thing,
Something he pities.
Something to possess.
He doesn't see you as equal.

He feels like God.

(But the difference between the boy and God is,
God made us in his image,
But the boy can't even see his reflection in your eyes...)

Thinks there is power at his fingertips,
And it is only his.
He is heavy with pride.

He wants you to need only him,
To see only him,
He wants you to forget who you are.
Wants you write his name in your Bible,
Wants you to write it in every holy text.

The boy will never need you,

He only wants you to beg for him.

Haunted Houses Look a Lot Like People

Sometimes you will think that the pain has disappeared.
Hallelujah you've been saved.
Thank the gods,
The hurt is gone…

Telling yourself that you don't miss him anymore.
I don't miss him,
I don't miss him.
I think I might miss-...
No, I don't miss him.

And the pain of him is usually good at staying gone.
Mostly because people like us are good at burying things.
But some things can only stay dead for so long.

But,

Memories of him?
They dig themselves out of their own graves.
Standing on the steps,
Ring, ring,
Ringing my heart shaped doorbell,
Mistaking my body for a haunted house.

But how many skeletons can a girl keep in her closet,
Before she starts going to battle wearing a skull for a helmet,
And a ribcage for armor?

And how many ghosts can she harbor,
Before she turns into one herself?

Then you realize that the pain was never really gone.
Just that you hadn't buried it deep enough.
We may be good at burying things.
But we aren't grave diggers.

And you start satisfying the ghosts with false hopes.
Maybe he will come back.

Maybe he did love you.

Start asking yourself,
Whether you're giving hope to the ghosts of the past,
Or the ghost you've become?

Because he's never coming back,
Not for you anyway.
And yes it hurts,
It hurts,
God it hurts.

But if you could do it over again,
Would you?

And the answer is always,
Yes,
Because you couldn't really help yourself.
He was always half ghost and half disaster.
And you were always better at being the haunted house.

Confessional

"Tell me you love me?" I know my eyes beg for it.
But I like to say it like a joke
He's not looking me in the eyes anyways.
Not really looking for the emotion.
Maybe he just doesn't want to see it, he doesn't say anything.
Just a grin and a head shake.
Just a joke right?

But I can feel the whole ocean collecting in my wide eyes.
If I open them further they won't water.
But then there's this blob in my throat,
Choking me.
Choking the ocean out as waterfalls.
Great heaving sobs want to rack the my whole body.
Lungs squeezing their own air out.

Just a joke.
Right?
Just a grin and a head shake,
Just a no.
"No I don't love you."

Broken Mechanics

I was born into this too tough world,
As a too soft thing.
And I know that sounds like every teenage melodramatic quote on
the face of the earth, but I mean it.
I tend to love a little too fast, and feel everything a little too fully.
A spun glass house in a world full of diamond hard edges.

There is a boy, that would be easy to love.
But there is no possibility of him loving me,
I am only a source of knowledge to him.
An always open book.
And he only wants me to spew out
information for him to devour.

Even if there was that smallest possibility,
I would not ask him to love me,
Would not ask any others to love me.
This sounds terribly sad but I'm doing them a justice.
Doing myself one in the process.
I will not make my struggle theirs.

This is mine to bare,
And my family's as well.
But I see their struggle.
And I'm scared to give that to another.
I've watched too many movies, heard too many stories.
And eventually they will want someone more human than me.
They will want more than what I can give them.
It will be easy for them to get.
I am less than half of a full.
I am only an imaginative brain and mouth and eyes.
Attached to immobile parts.
An engine, with broken mechanics.

Part Five:

On endings

Small Absolutes

I firmly believe there are some small things in this world.
Small things that feel like tiny forevers.
Small things that are absolutely meant to happen.

Tiny forevers that make psychics and palm readers smile when they
see yours.
Tiny forever that taste like snowflakes.
Tiny forevers like his eyes.

Small things,
Tiny, unforgettable forevers,
That mean the whole damn world.

Shipwrecks and Salt Water

I'm here to tell you that surviving,
Doesn't always feel like surviving.

Sometimes it feels less like winning,
And more like wound,
And wound and wound.
And a sinking ship.
It sounds like wreckage.

I'm here to tell you that the Captain,
Doesn't have to sink with the ship.
You are not drowning,
You are only learning how to swim,
And I promise that you can do it.

www.ingramcontent.com/pod-product-compliance
Lightning Source LLC
Chambersburg PA
CBHW071317200626
46813CB00015B/2249